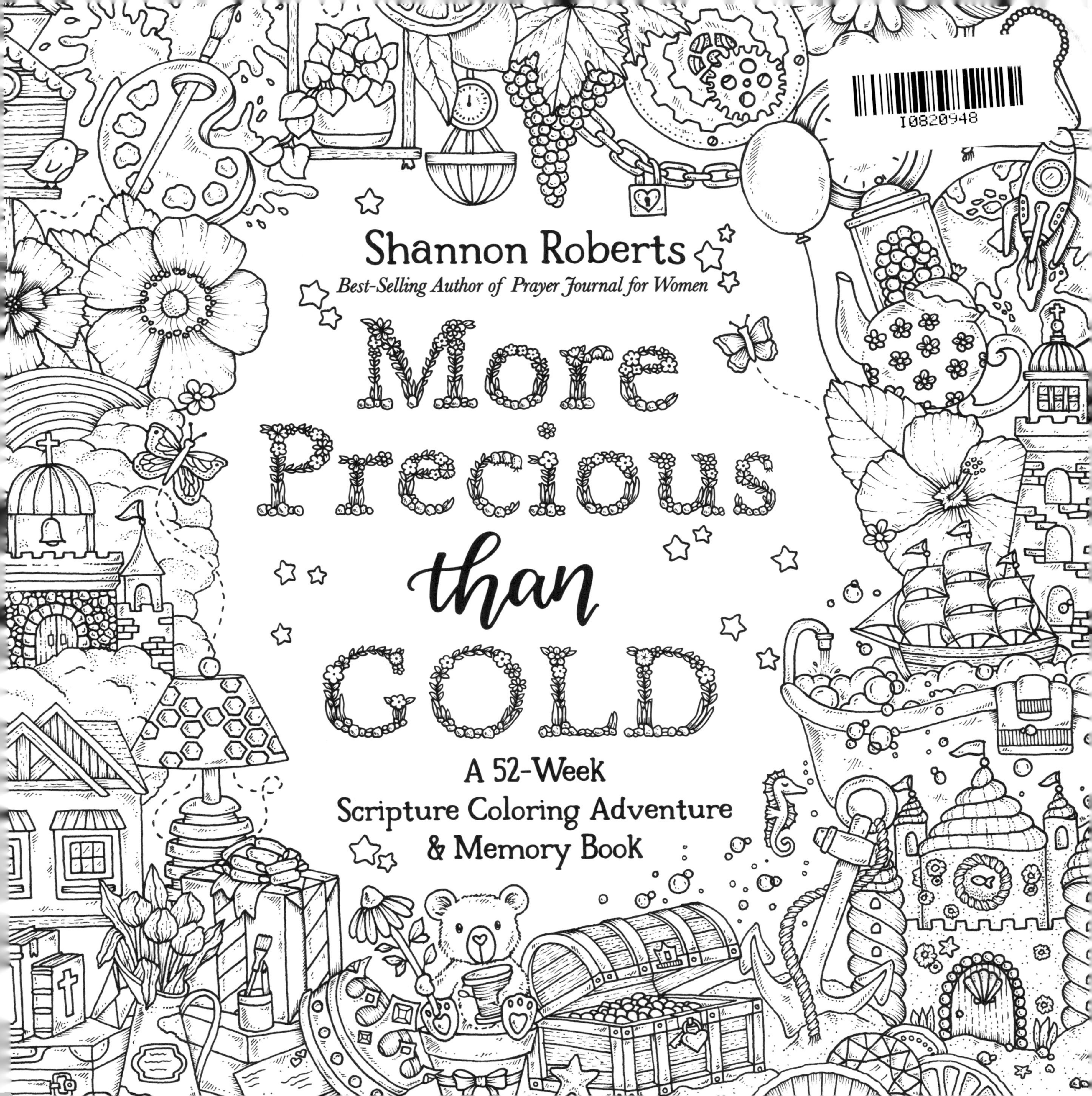
Shannon Roberts
Best-Selling Author of Prayer Journal for Women
More Precious than GOLD
A 52-Week
Scripture Coloring Adventure
& Memory Book
I0820948

To the people in my life *more precious than gold*—my family. John, Skylar, Asher, & Baylor, I love, cherish, and thank God for you! Thank you for your love, support, and patience as I created the pages of this book. You inspire me!

Visit Christian Art Gifts, Inc., at www.christianartgifts.com.

More Precious than Gold: A 52-Week Scripture Coloring Adventure and Memory Book

Published by Christian Art Gifts, Inc., Bloomingdale, IL, USA.

First edition 2025.

Written, designed, and illustrated by Shannon Roberts.

ISBN 979-8-89678-229-2

Printed in China.

30 29 28 27 26 25
10 9 8 7 6 5 4 3 2 1

This Book Belongs To

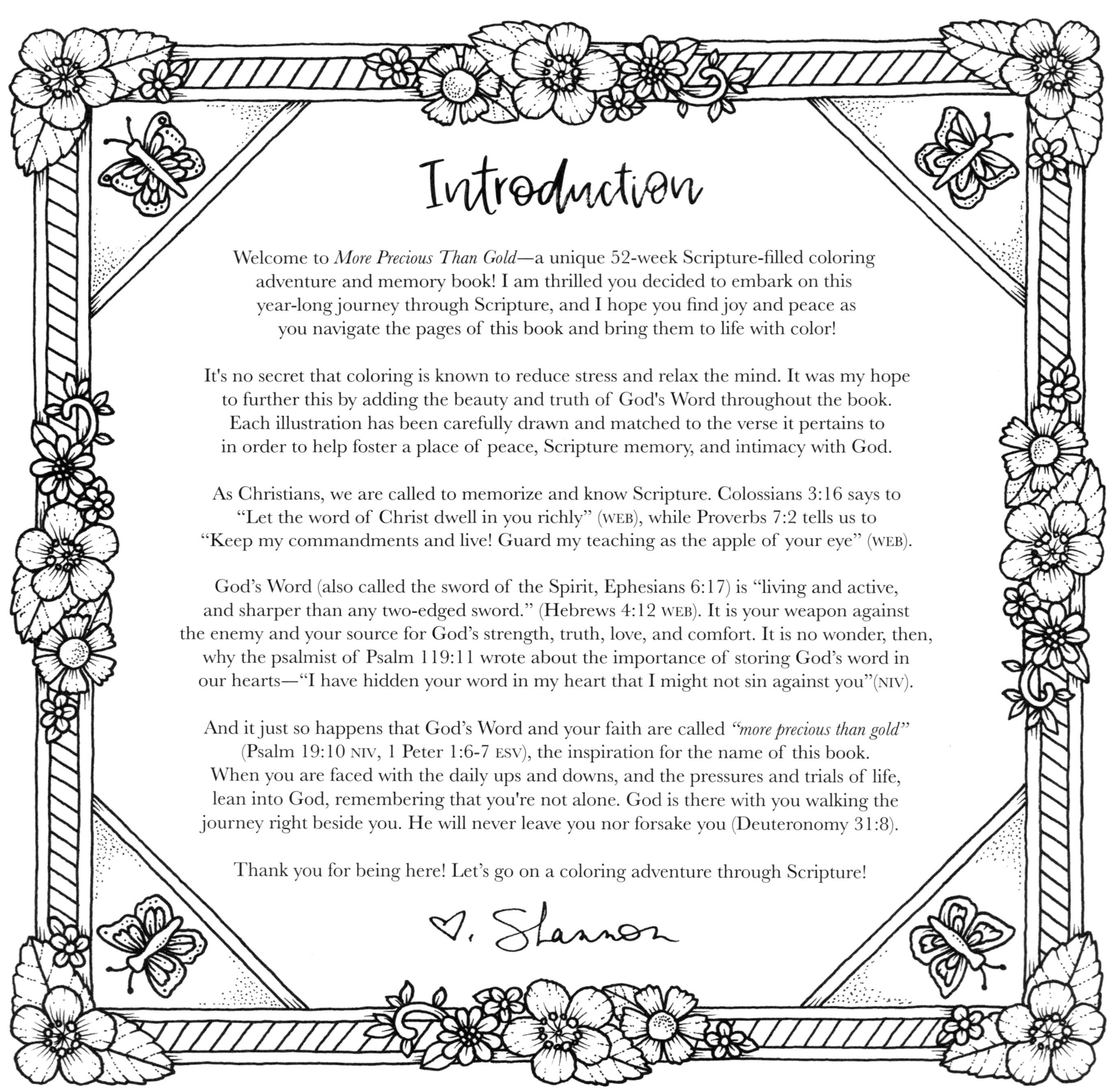

Introduction

Welcome to *More Precious Than Gold*—a unique 52-week Scripture-filled coloring adventure and memory book! I am thrilled you decided to embark on this year-long journey through Scripture, and I hope you find joy and peace as you navigate the pages of this book and bring them to life with color!

It's no secret that coloring is known to reduce stress and relax the mind. It was my hope to further this by adding the beauty and truth of God's Word throughout the book. Each illustration has been carefully drawn and matched to the verse it pertains to in order to help foster a place of peace, Scripture memory, and intimacy with God.

As Christians, we are called to memorize and know Scripture. Colossians 3:16 says to "Let the word of Christ dwell in you richly" (WEB), while Proverbs 7:2 tells us to "Keep my commandments and live! Guard my teaching as the apple of your eye" (WEB).

God's Word (also called the sword of the Spirit, Ephesians 6:17) is "living and active, and sharper than any two-edged sword." (Hebrews 4:12 WEB). It is your weapon against the enemy and your source for God's strength, truth, love, and comfort. It is no wonder, then, why the psalmist of Psalm 119:11 wrote about the importance of storing God's word in our hearts—"I have hidden your word in my heart that I might not sin against you"(NIV).

And it just so happens that God's Word and your faith are called *"more precious than gold"* (Psalm 19:10 NIV, 1 Peter 1:6-7 ESV), the inspiration for the name of this book. When you are faced with the daily ups and downs, and the pressures and trials of life, lean into God, remembering that you're not alone. God is there with you walking the journey right beside you. He will never leave you nor forsake you (Deuteronomy 31:8).

Thank you for being here! Let's go on a coloring adventure through Scripture!

♡, Shannon

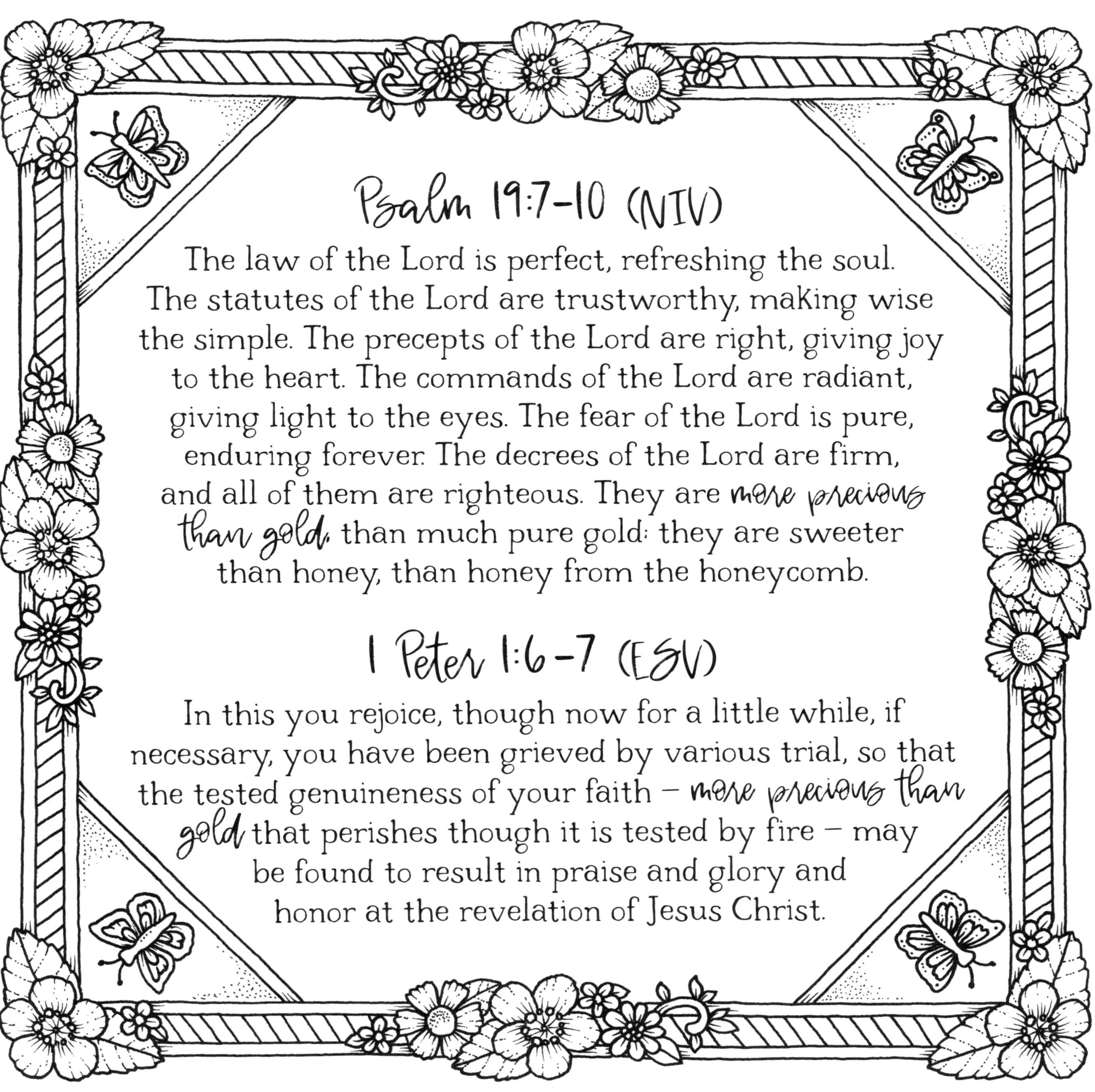

Psalm 19:7-10 (NIV)

The law of the Lord is perfect, refreshing the soul. The statutes of the Lord are trustworthy, making wise the simple. The precepts of the Lord are right, giving joy to the heart. The commands of the Lord are radiant, giving light to the eyes. The fear of the Lord is pure, enduring forever. The decrees of the Lord are firm, and all of them are righteous. They are *more precious than gold,* than much pure gold; they are sweeter than honey, than honey from the honeycomb.

1 Peter 1:6-7 (ESV)

In this you rejoice, though now for a little while, if necessary, you have been grieved by various trial, so that the tested genuineness of your faith – *more precious than gold* that perishes though it is tested by fire – may be found to result in praise and glory and honor at the revelation of Jesus Christ.

Table of Contents

Old Testament - • New Testament - ◦

Scripture Tips

- Focus on *one* verse per week. This will give you time to fully memorize and color each verse.

- Try to memorize the calligraphy key word(s) for each verse, as this will also help with memory retention.

- After memorizing and coloring a verse, check off the box ☐ in the table of contents so you know that you have completed it. Be sure to revisit the verses you've memorized throughout the year!

- Try to recite each verse multiple times as you color, whether out loud or in your head. This repetition will help you remember it.

- Feel free to go in the order of the book or skip around to different verses according to your own needs and wants.

- If you can, team up with others to memorize and color the Scriptures together! This helps connect you with your brothers and sisters in Christ and hold each other accountable.

Coloring Tips

❁ Colored pencils are recommended, but be cautious of markers and coloring mediums involving ink as there is a higher possibility of ink bleeding through to the other side of the page. Before coloring, test each color on the color test pages in the back of the book.

❁ If you are feeling overwhelmed by the details of a particular design, take a break and come back to it. Oftentimes, you'll be excited to pick up where you left off!

❁ Share your coloring creations on social media! Use the hashtag #MorePreciousThanGoldBook and tag me @shannonroberts19 for a chance to have your coloring page(s) featured!

❁ For more information about this book including retailers and coloring tips, be sure to visit my website shannonroberts.com.

#MorePreciousThanGoldBook
@shannonroberts19

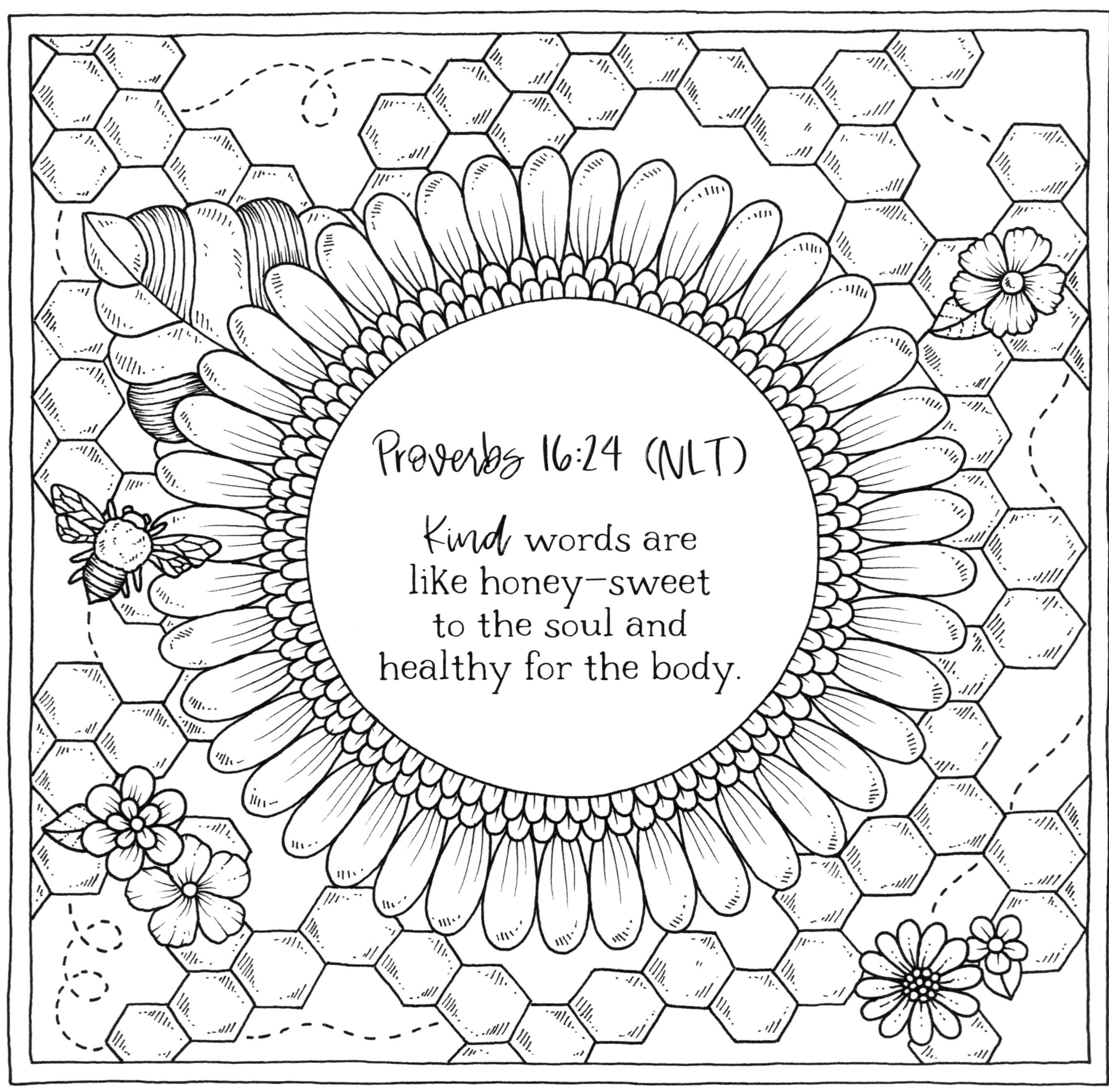
Proverbs 16:24 (NLT)
Kind words are
like honey—sweet
to the soul and
healthy for the body.

KINDNESS

Hebrews 6:19 (NIV)

We have this *hope* as
an anchor for the soul,
firm and secure.

HOPE
N
E
S
W

Psalm 139:13-14 (WEB)
For you formed my inmost
being. You knit me together
in my mother's womb. I will
give thanks to you, for I am
fearfully and wonderfully
made. Your works are
wonderful. My soul
knows that very well.

WONDERFUL

Your word is a lamp
to my feet and
a *light* for my path.

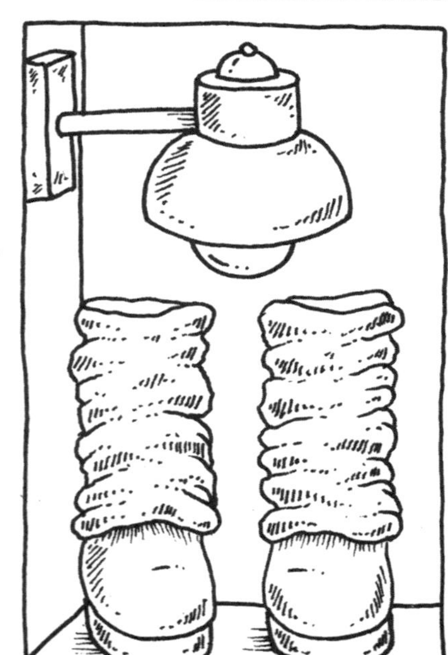

Light

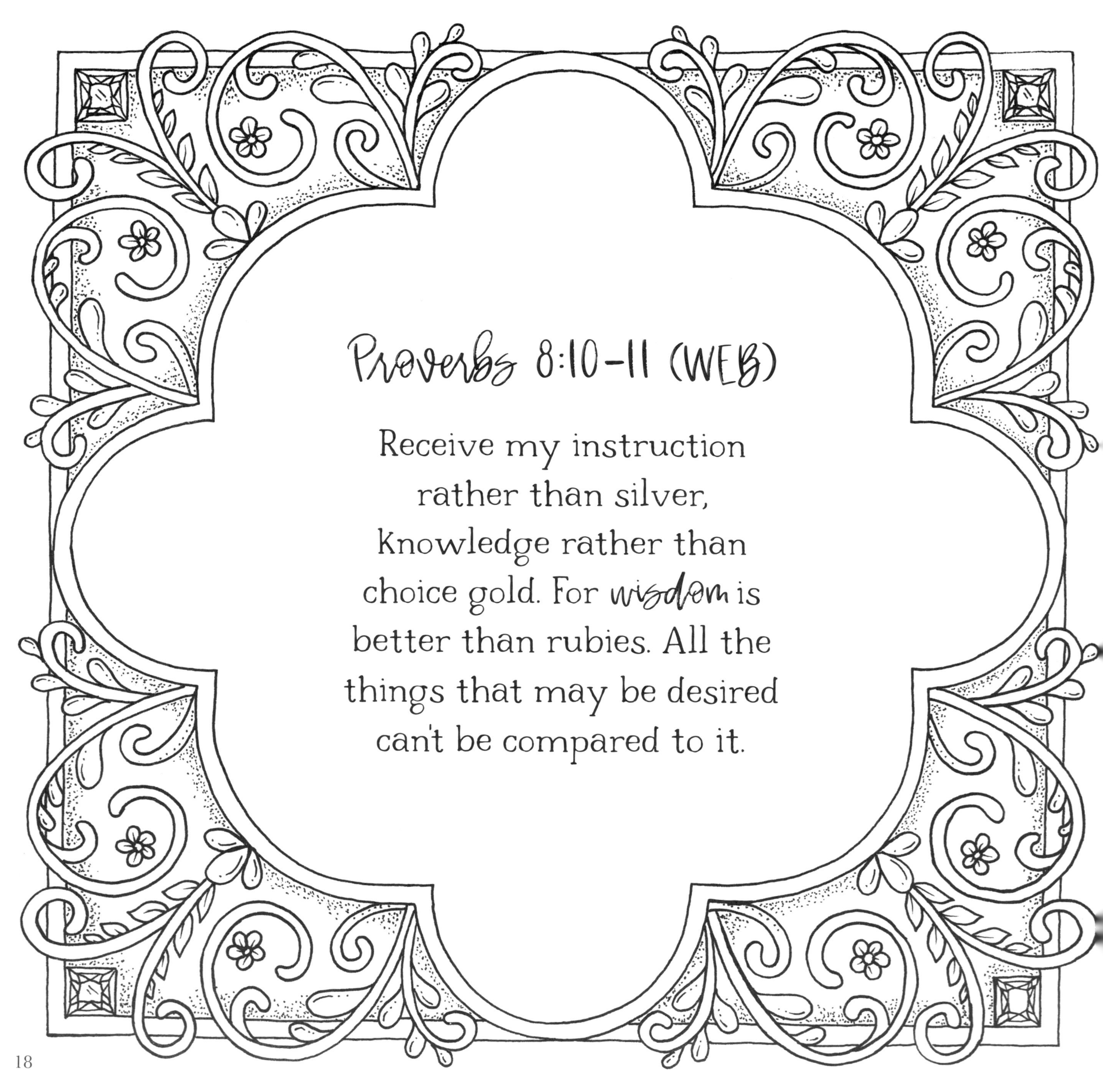
Proverbs 8:10-11 (WEB)
Receive my instruction
rather than silver,
Knowledge rather than
choice gold. For wisdom is
better than rubies. All the
things that may be desired
can't be compared to it.

WISDOM

Ecclesiastes 3:11 (NIV)
He has made everything
beautiful in its time. He has
also set eternity in the
human heart; yet no one
can fathom what God has
done from beginning to end.

Beautiful

Jeremiah 29:13 (WEB)
You shall seek me and find
me, when you search for
me with all your heart.

HEART

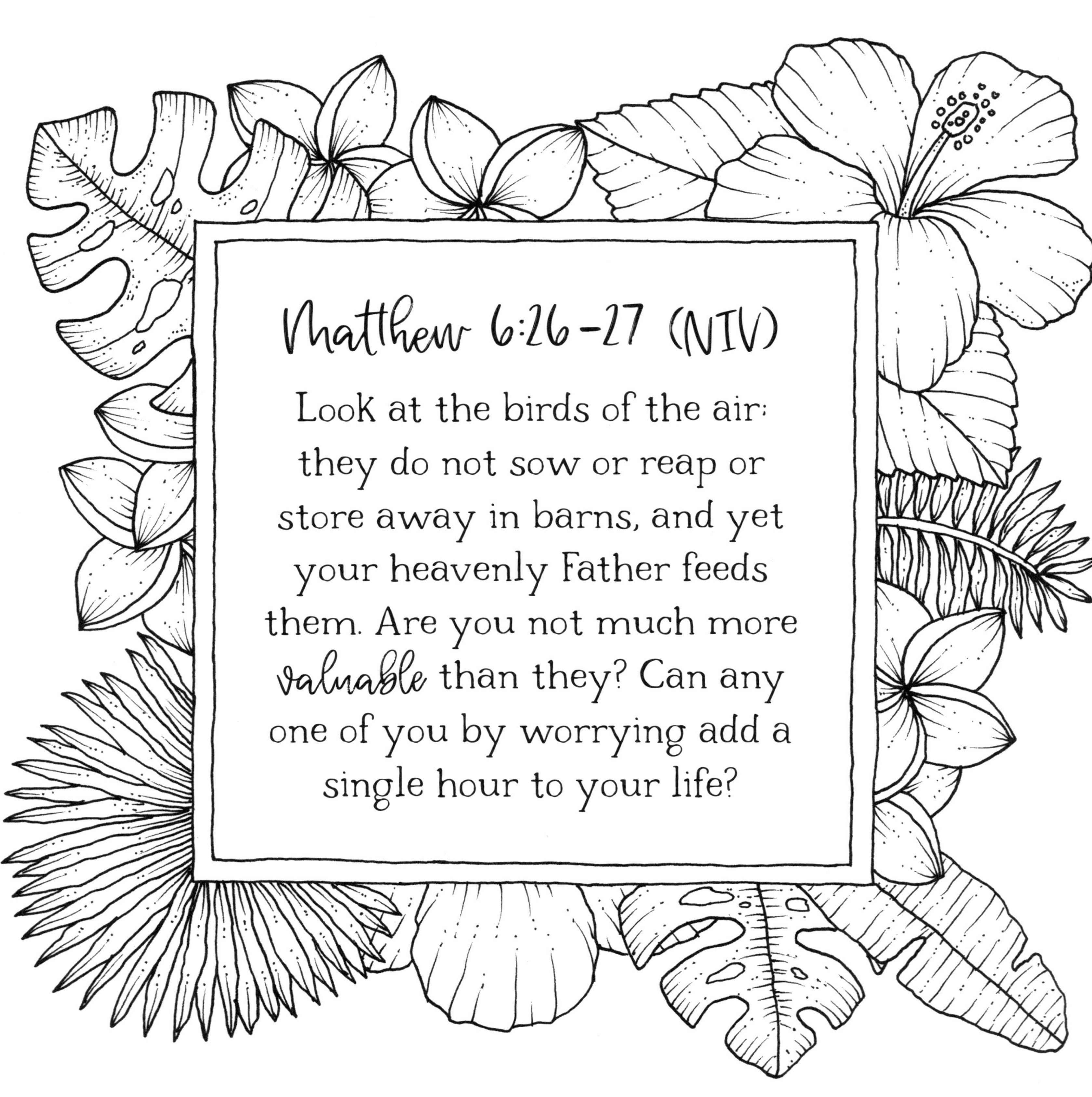
Matthew 6:26-27 (NIV)
Look at the birds of the air:
they do not sow or reap or
store away in barns, and yet
your heavenly Father feeds
them. Are you not much more
valuable than they? Can any
one of you by worrying add a
single hour to your life?

VALUABLE

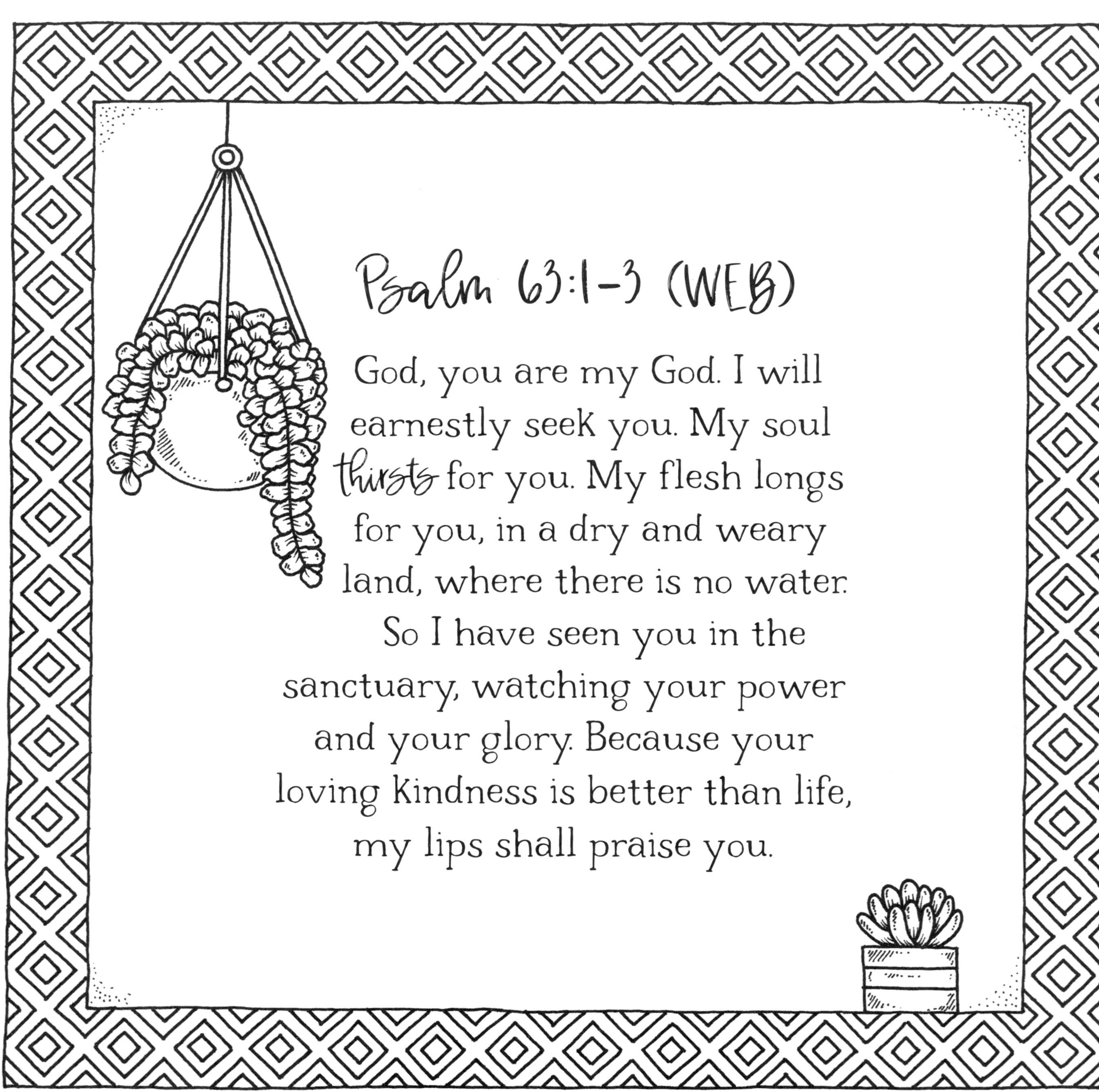
Psalm 63:1-3 (WEB)
God, you are my God. I will
earnestly seek you. My soul
thirsts for you. My flesh longs
for you, in a dry and weary
land, where there is no water.
So I have seen you in the
sanctuary, watching your power
and your glory. Because your
loving kindness is better than life,
my lips shall praise you.

thirsty

Galatians 5:22-23 (ESV)

But the fruit of the Spirit is love, joy, peace, patience, kindness, goodness, faithfulness, gentleness, self-control; against such things there is no law.

FRUIT
LOVE
JOY
PEACE
PATIENCE
KINDNESS
GOODNESS
FAITHFULNESS
GENTLENESS
SELF-CONTROL

N
W
E
S
Matthew 6:19-21 (ESV)
Do not lay up for yourselves treasures on earth, where moth and rust destroy and where thieves break in and steal, but lay up for yourselves treasures in heaven, where neither moth nor rust destroys and where thieves do not break in and steal. For where your treasure is, there your heart will be also.

TREASURE
HOLY
Bible

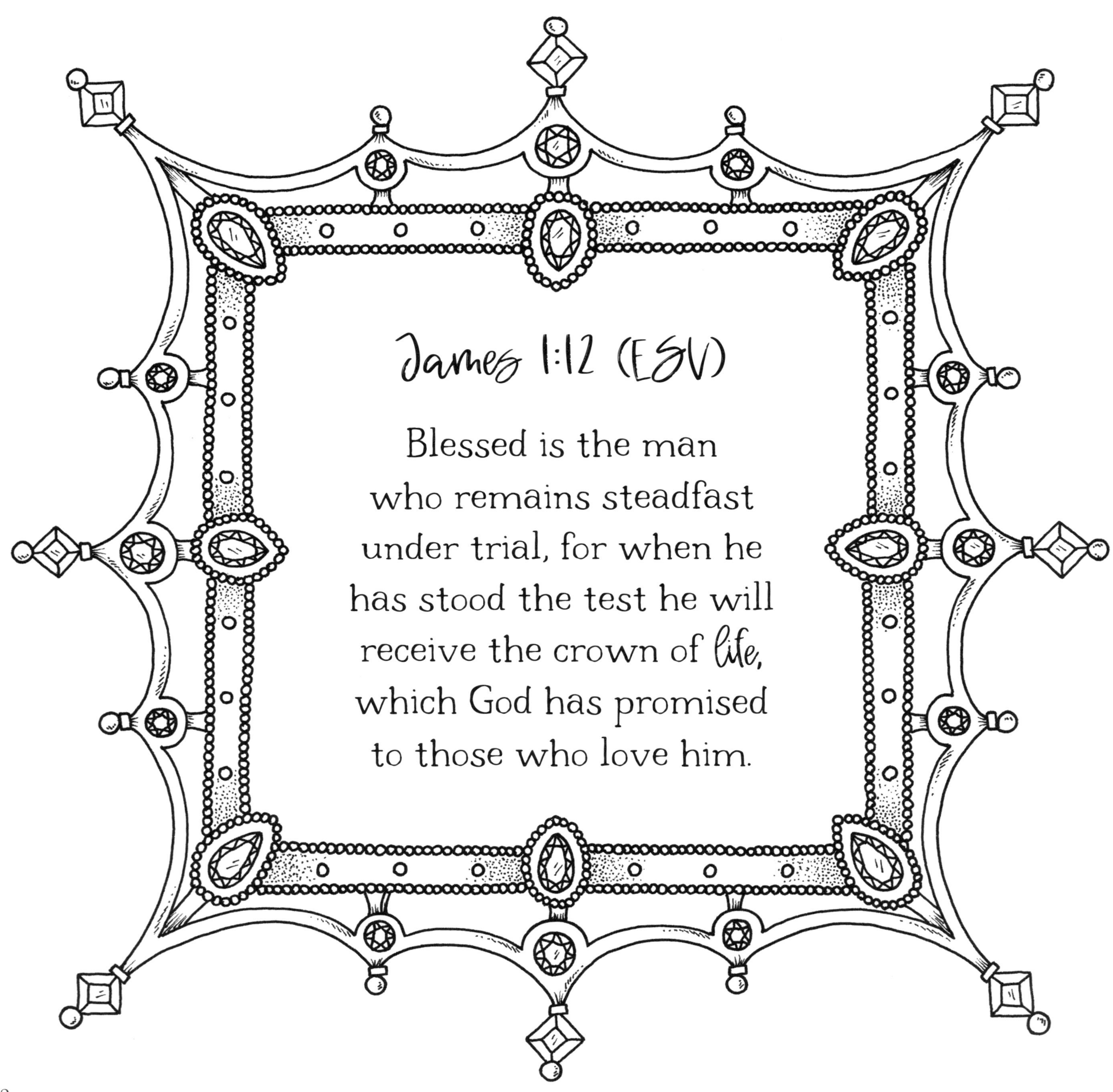
James 1:12 (ESV)
Blessed is the man
who remains steadfast
under trial, for when he
has stood the test he will
receive the crown of life,
which God has promised
to those who love him.

LIFE

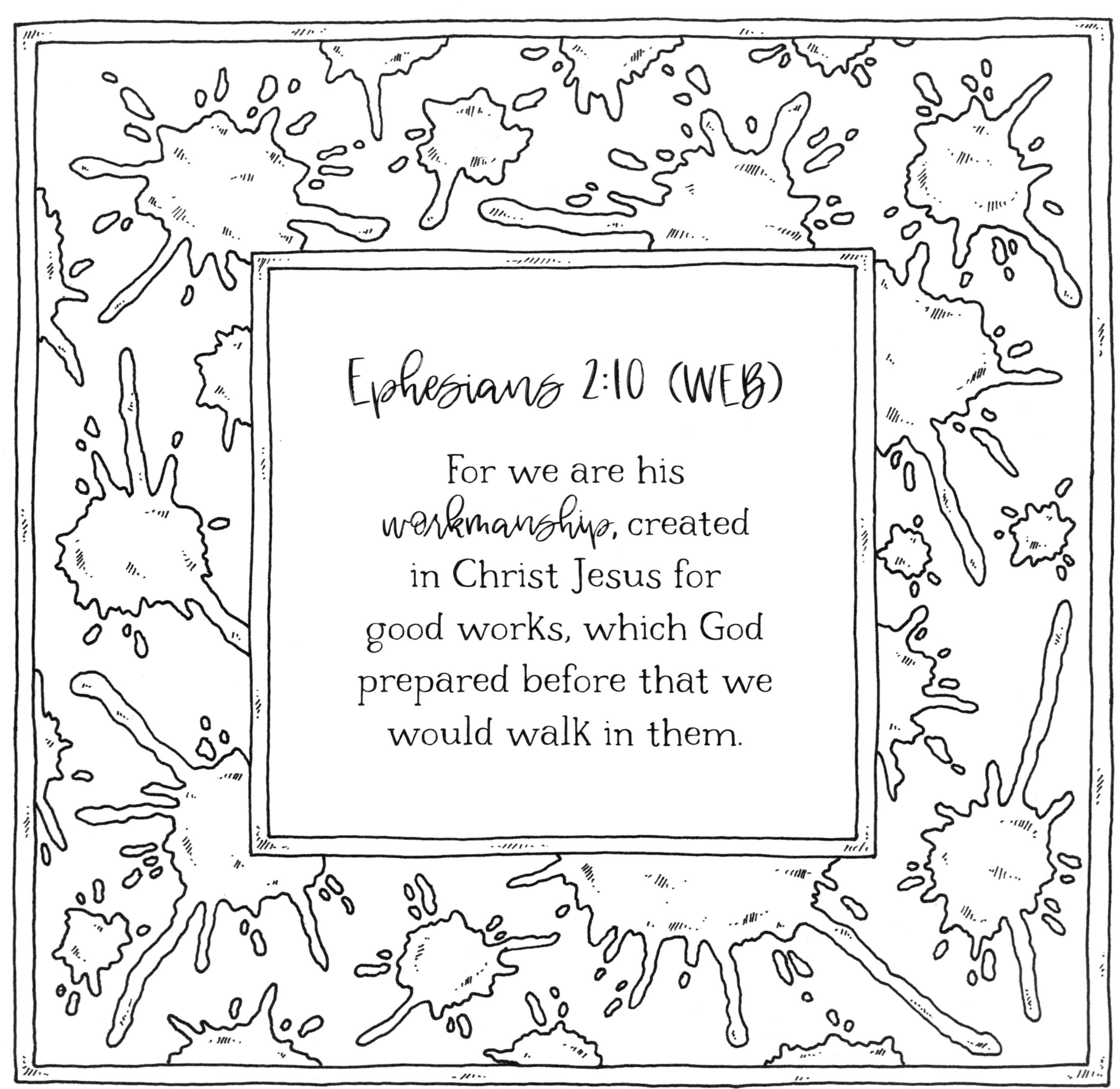
Ephesians 2:10 (WEB)
For we are his
workmanship, created
in Christ Jesus for
good works, which God
prepared before that we
would walk in them.

WORKMANSHIP

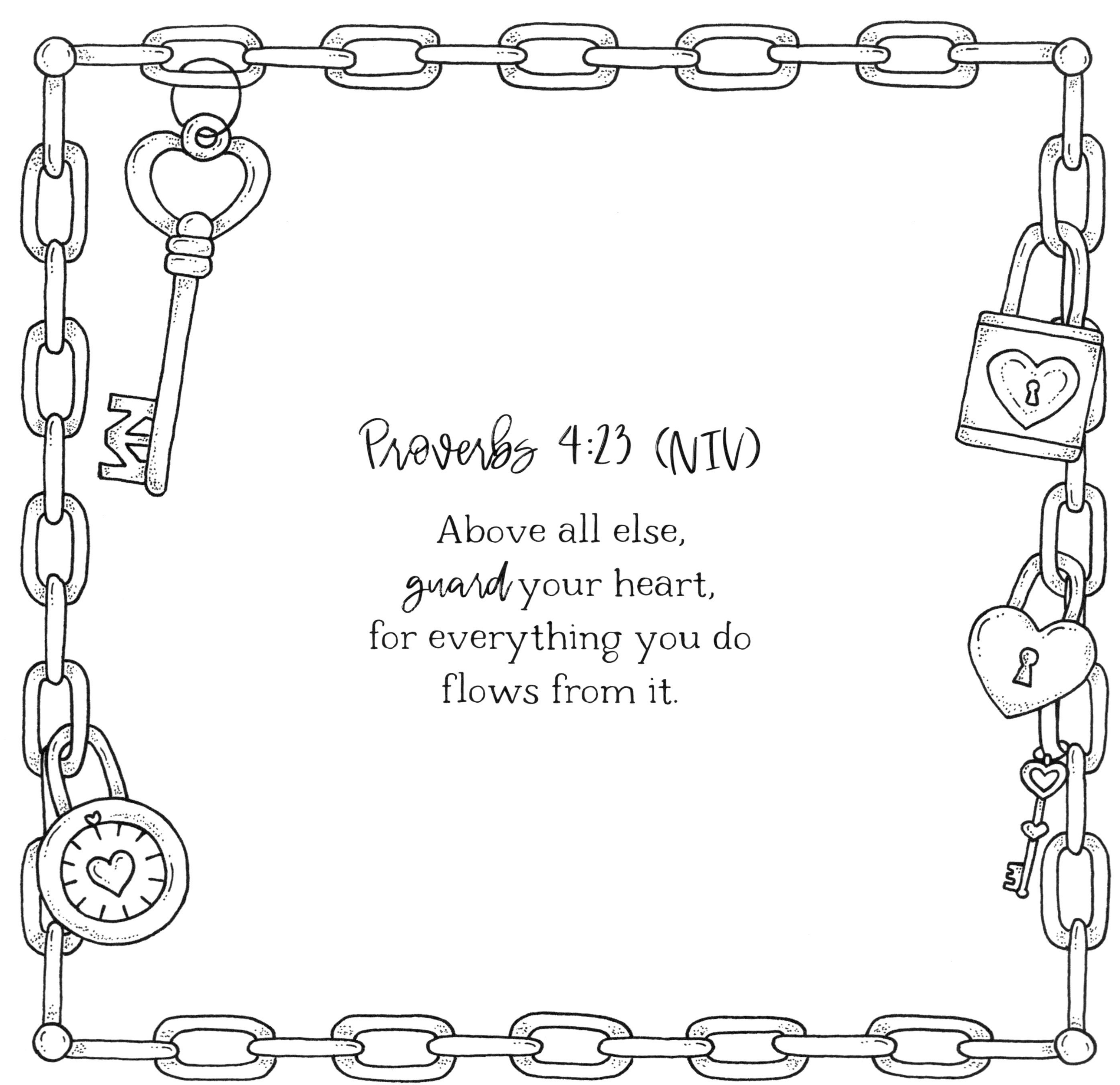
Proverbs 4:23 (NIV)
Above all else,
guard your heart,
for everything you do
flows from it.

GUARD
MY

Isaiah 26:3 (ESV)
You keep him in perfect
peace whose mind is stayed
on you, because he
trusts in you.

PEACE

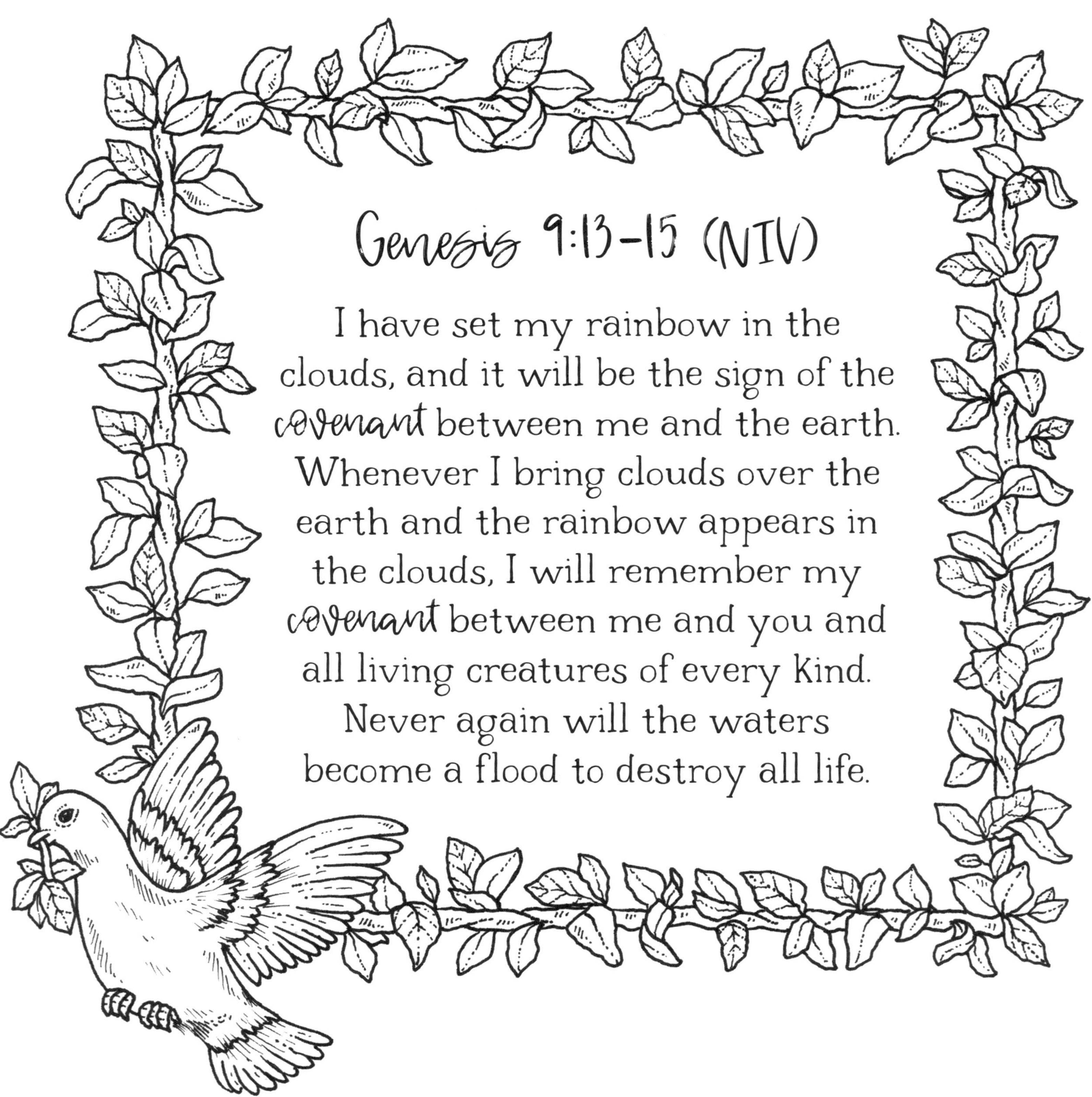

Genesis 9:13–15 (NIV)

I have set my rainbow in the clouds, and it will be the sign of the *covenant* between me and the earth. Whenever I bring clouds over the earth and the rainbow appears in the clouds, I will remember my *covenant* between me and you and all living creatures of every kind. Never again will the waters become a flood to destroy all life.

covenant

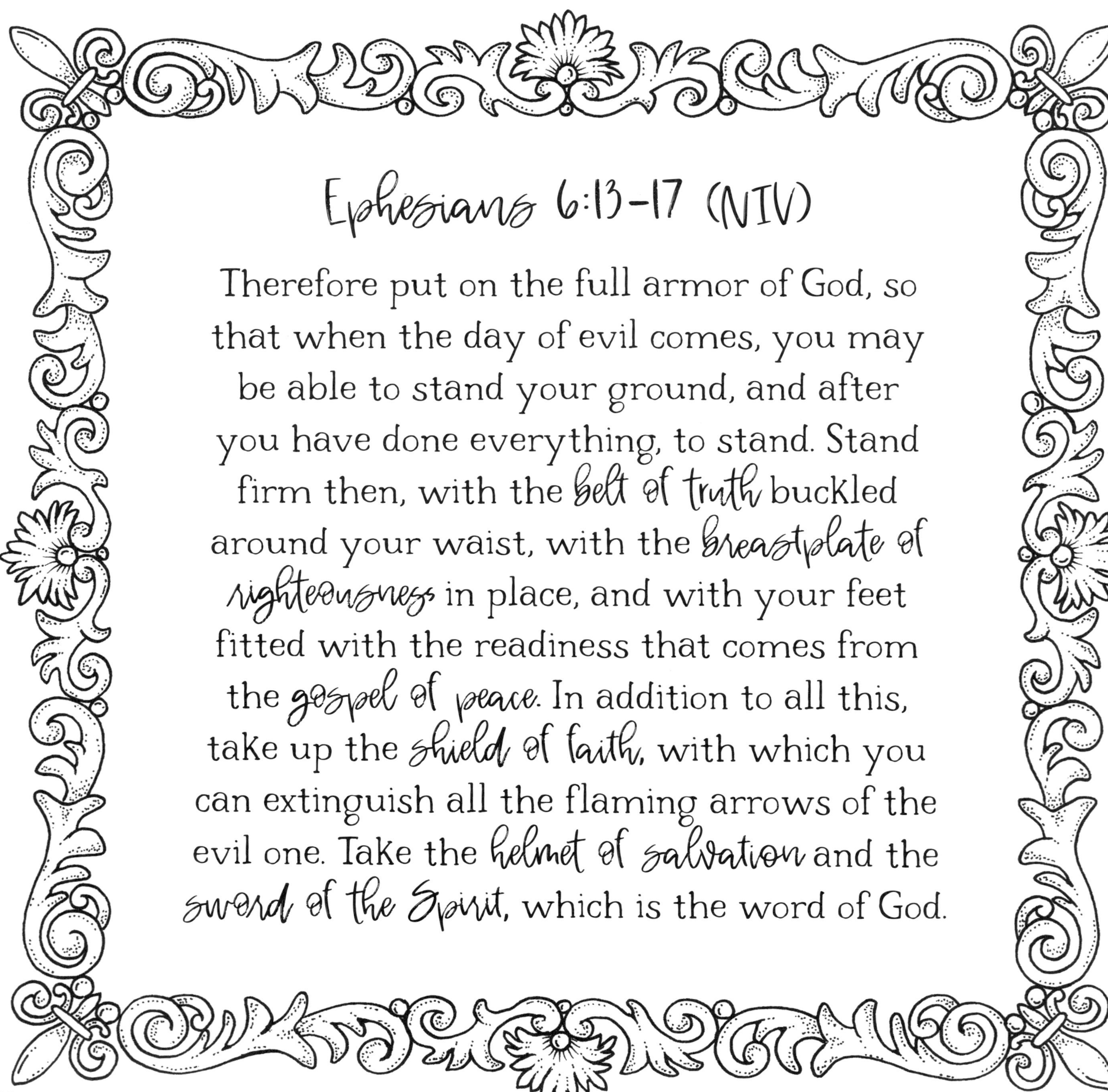

Ephesians 6:13-17 (NIV)

Therefore put on the full armor of God, so that when the day of evil comes, you may be able to stand your ground, and after you have done everything, to stand. Stand firm then, with the belt of truth buckled around your waist, with the breastplate of righteousness in place, and with your feet fitted with the readiness that comes from the gospel of peace. In addition to all this, take up the shield of faith, with which you can extinguish all the flaming arrows of the evil one. Take the helmet of salvation and the sword of the Spirit, which is the word of God.

ARMOR
TRUTH
RIGHTEOUSNESS
GOSPEL OF PEACE
FAITH
HOLY BIBLE
SALVATION
SPIRIT

To: You
With Love,
God
James 1:17 (WEB)
Every good gift and every
perfect gift is from above,
coming down from the
Father of lights, with
whom can be no variation,
nor turning shadow.

Joshua 1:9 (NLT)
This is my command—be
strong and courageous!
Do not be afraid or
discouraged. For the Lord
your God is with you
wherever you go.

COURAGE
GOD
IS
WITH
YOU

Proverbs 31:25 (ESV)
Strength and dignity are her
clothing, and she laughs
at the time to come.

dignity

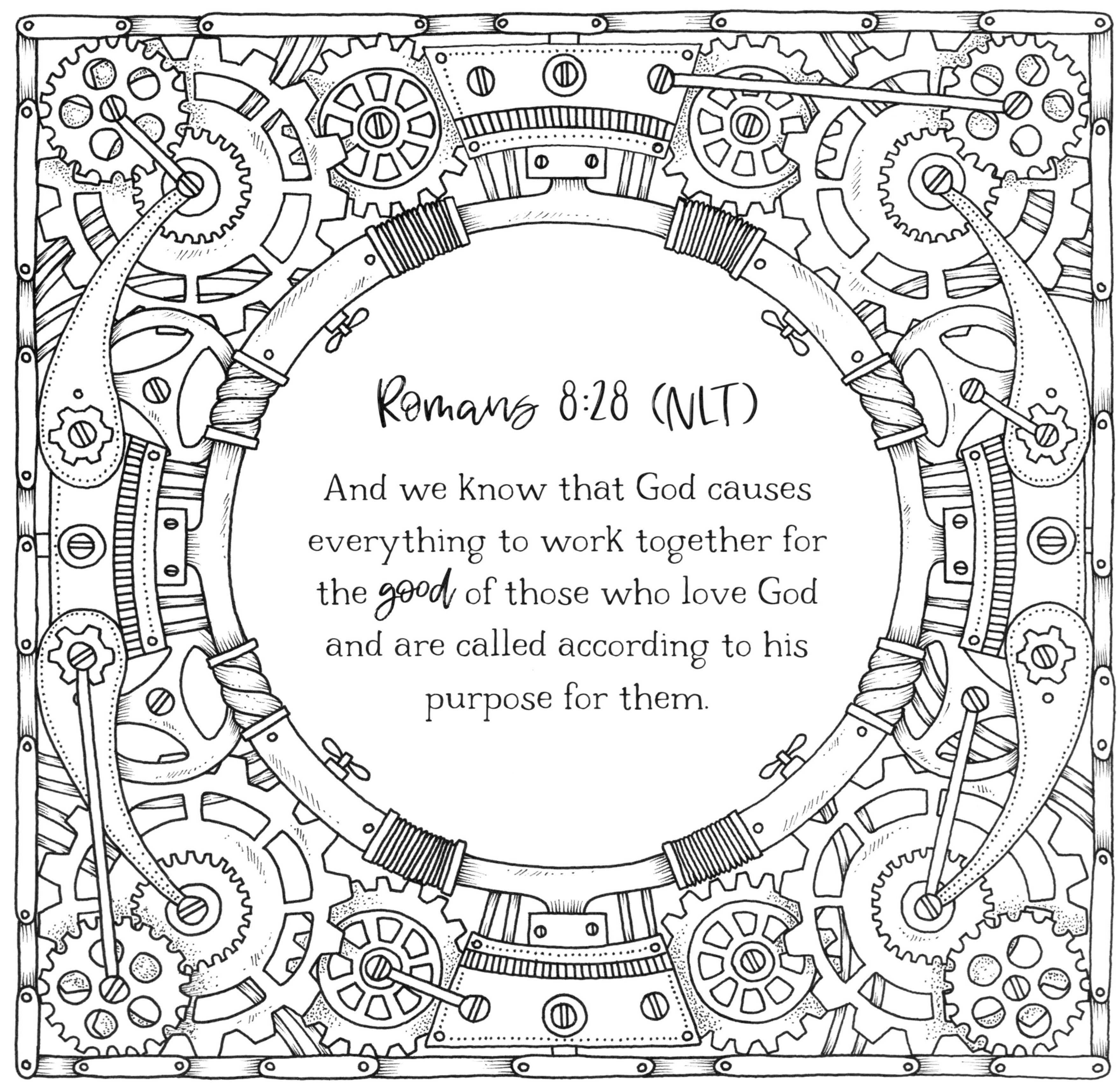
Romans 8:28 (NLT)
And we know that God causes everything to work together for the good of those who love God and are called according to his purpose for them.

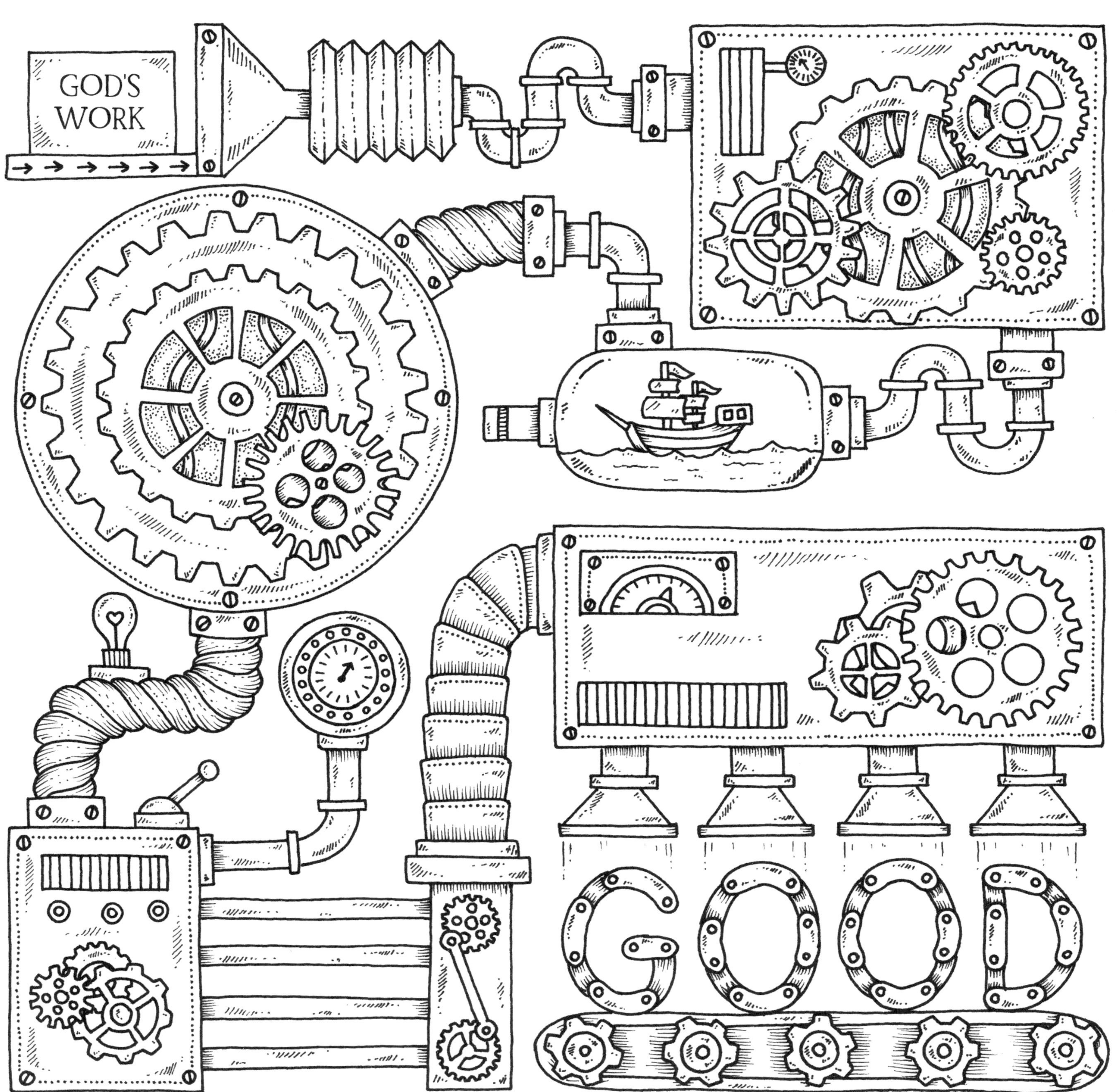
GOD'S WORK
GOOD

GOD.AID
GOD.AID
GOD.AID
GOD.AID
Psalm 147:3 (WEB)
He heals the broken
in heart, and binds
up their wounds.

heals

2 Corinthians 5:17 (WEB)
Therefore if anyone is in
Christ, he is a new creation.
The old things have passed
away. Behold, all things
have become new.

NEW

I John 1:9 (WEB)
If we confess our sins, he is faithful
and righteous to forgive us
the sins and to cleanse us
from all unrighteousness.

CLEANSE

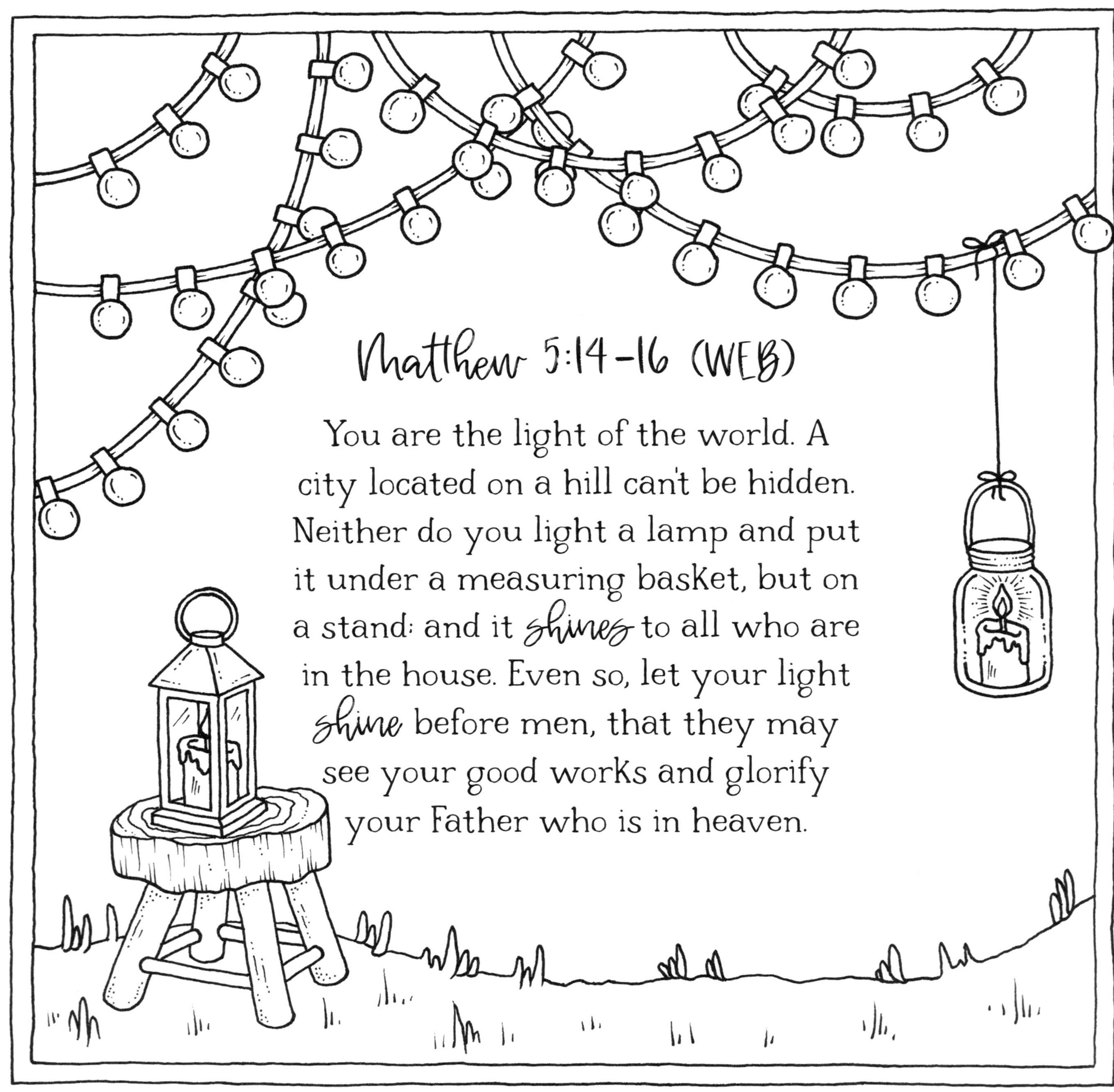
Matthew 5:14-16 (WEB)
You are the light of the world. A
city located on a hill can't be hidden.
Neither do you light a lamp and put
it under a measuring basket, but on
a stand; and it shines to all who are
in the house. Even so, let your light
shine before men, that they may
see your good works and glorify
your Father who is in heaven.

shine

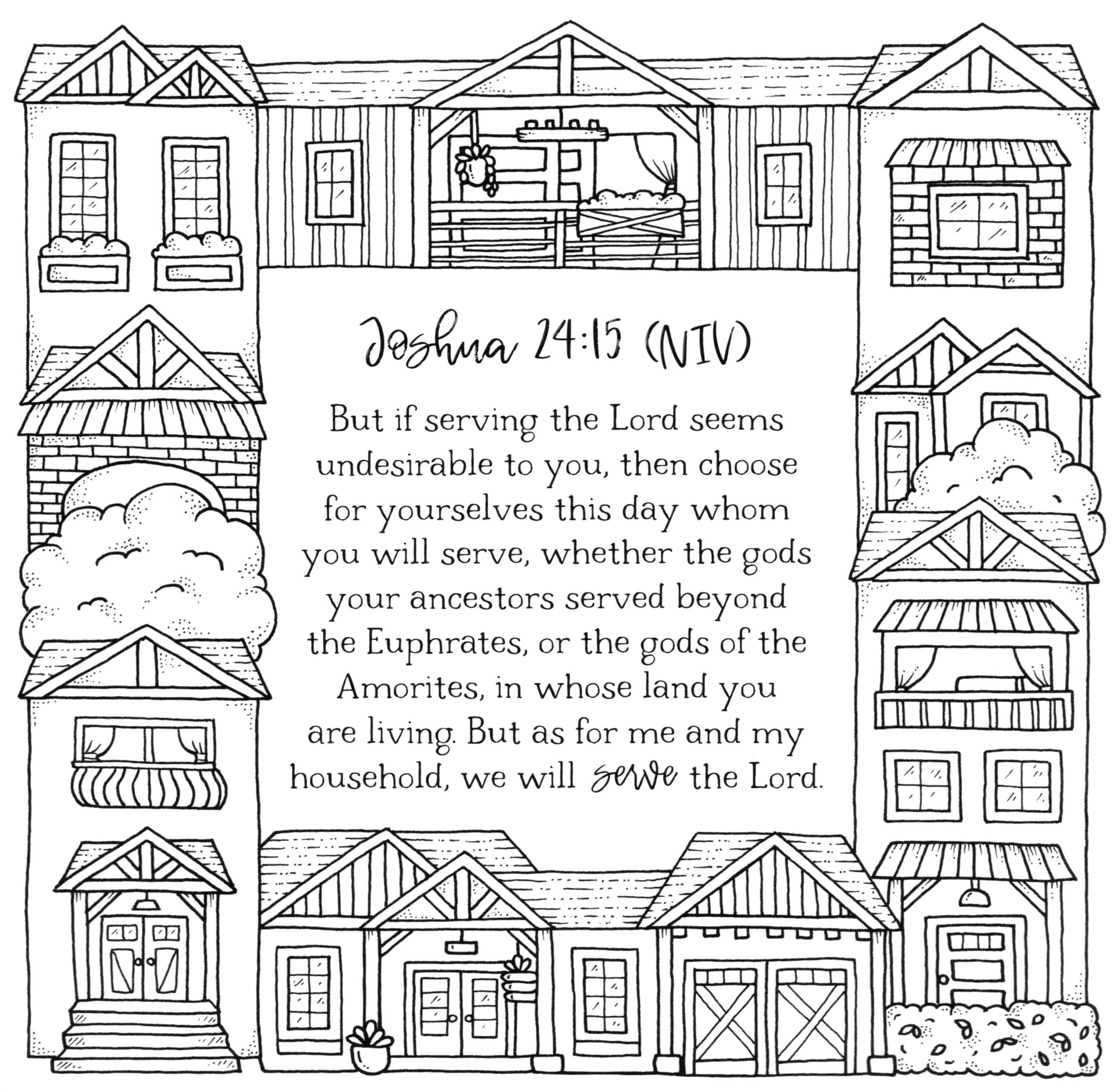
Joshua 24:15 (NIV)
But if serving the Lord seems undesirable to you, then choose for yourselves this day whom you will serve, whether the gods your ancestors served beyond the Euphrates, or the gods of the Amorites, in whose land you are living. But as for me and my household, we will serve the Lord.

SERVE

EXIT
1 Corinthians 10:13 (NIV)
No temptation has
overtaken you except
what is common to
mankind. And God is
faithful; he will not let
you be tempted
beyond what you can
bear. But when you are
tempted, he will also
provide a way out so
that you can endure it.

faithful

Psalm 91:1-4 (NLT)
Those who live in the shelter of
the Most High will find rest in the
shadow of the Almighty. This I declare
about the Lord: He alone is my refuge,
my place of safety; he is my God, and I
trust him. For he will rescue you from
every trap and protect you from deadly
disease. He will cover you with his
feathers. He will shelter you with
his wings. His faithful promises
are your armor and
protection.

Shelter

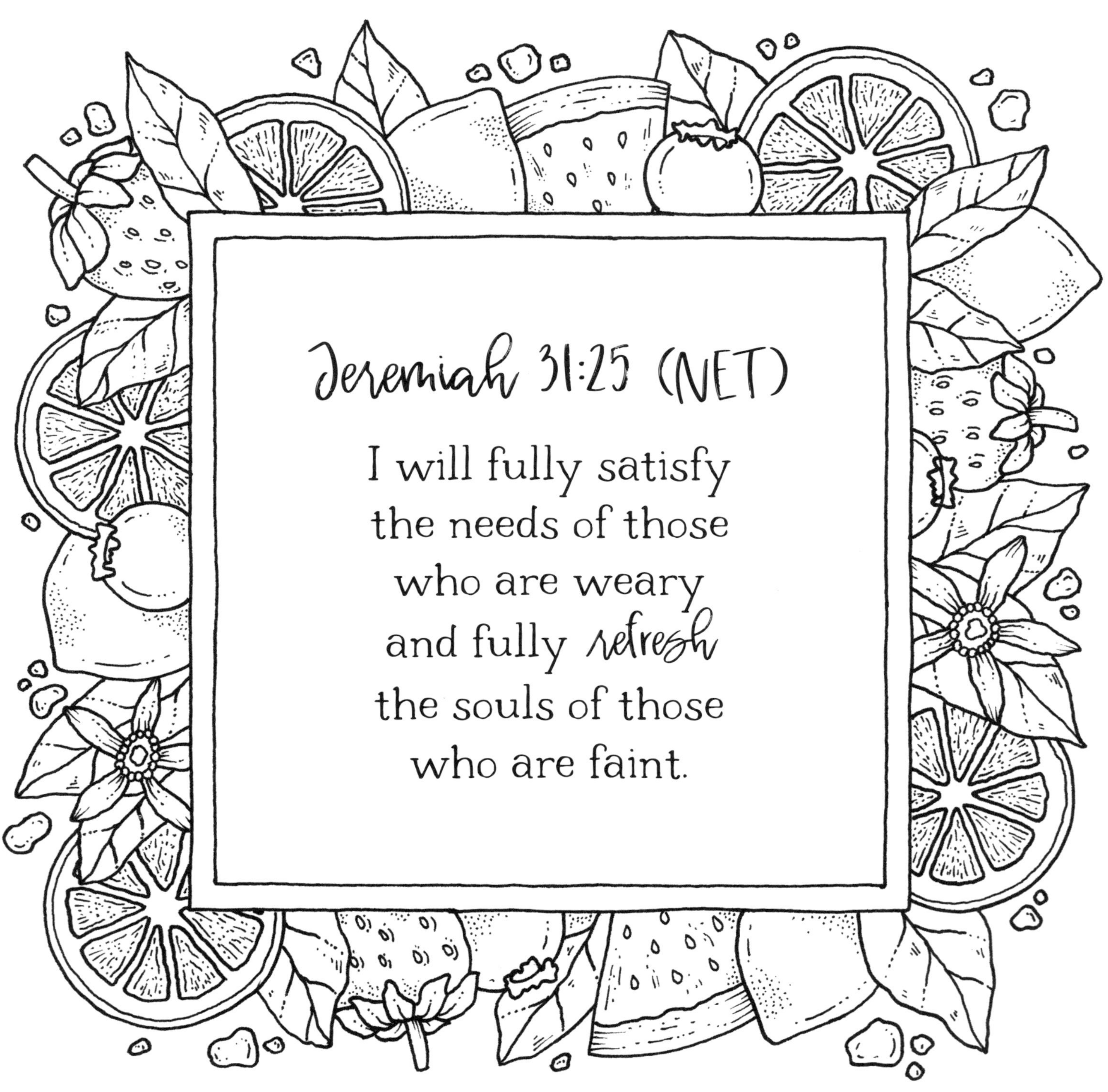
Jeremiah 31:25 (NET)
I will fully satisfy
the needs of those
who are weary
and fully refresh
the souls of those
who are faint.

refresh

Psalm 30:5 (WEB)
For his anger is but for a moment. His favor is for a lifetime. Weeping may stay for the night, but joy comes in the morning.

Joy

Isaiah 40:31 (NIV)
But those who hope
in the Lord will renew
their strength. They will
soar on wings like eagles;
they will run and not
grow weary, they will
walk and not be faint.

RENEW

1 Peter 3:3-4 (NIV)
Your beauty should not come from outward adornment, such as elaborate hairstyles and the wearing of gold jewelry or fine clothes. Rather, it should be that of your inner self, the unfading beauty of a gentle and quiet spirit, which is of great worth in God's sight.

unfading

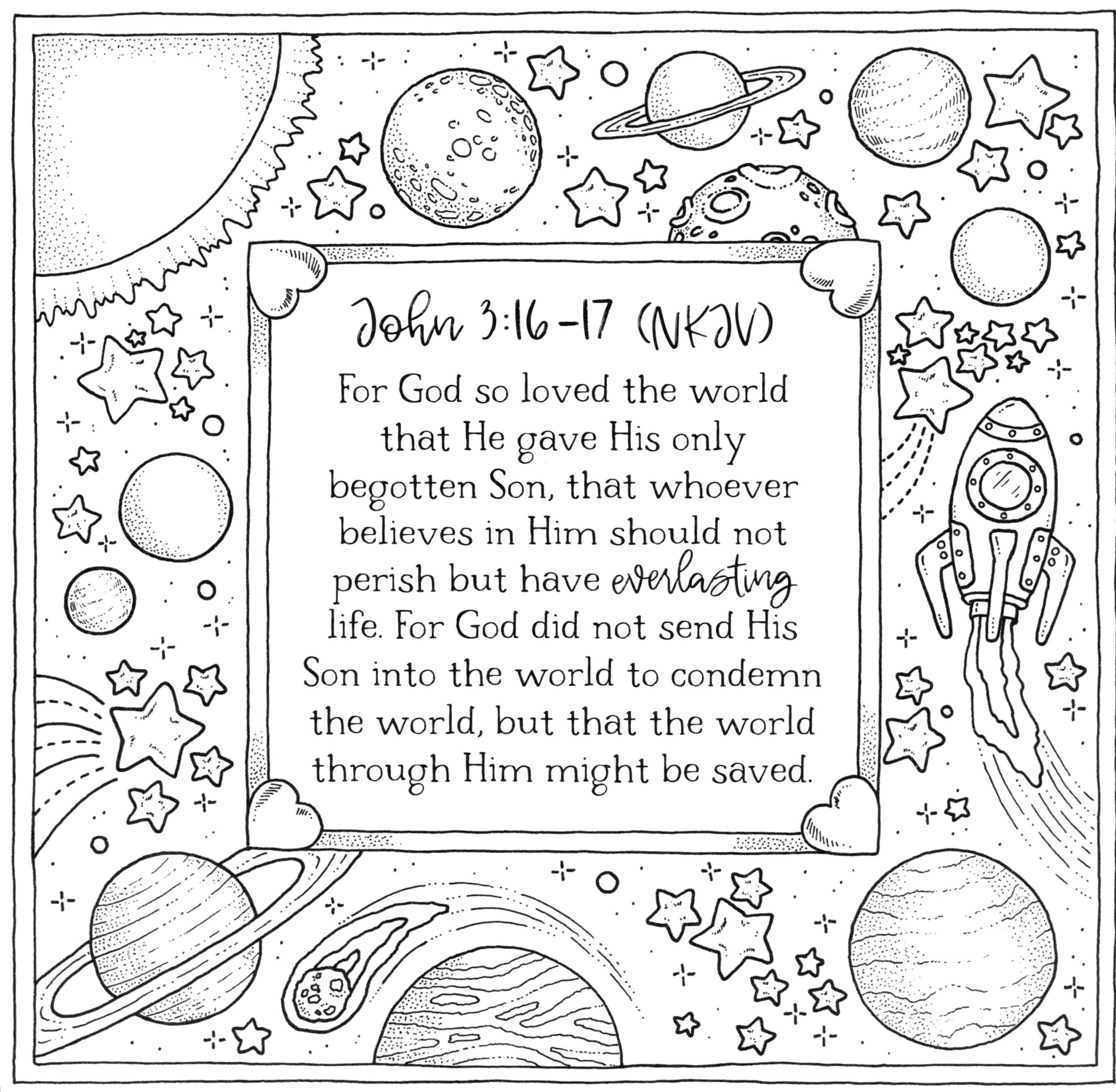
John 3:16–17 (NKJV)
For God so loved the world
that He gave His only
begotten Son, that whoever
believes in Him should not
perish but have everlasting
life. For God did not send His
Son into the world to condemn
the world, but that the world
through Him might be saved.

everlasting

12
1
2
3
4
5
6
7
8
9
10
11
2 Peter 3:8–9 (WEB)
But don't forget this one thing, beloved, that one day is with the Lord as a thousand years, and a thousand years as one day. The Lord is not slow concerning his promise, as some count slowness: but he is patient with us, not wishing that anyone should perish, but that all should come to repentance.

PATIENCE
12
1
2
3
4
5
6
7
8
9
10
11

1 Corinthians 13:4-7 (WEB)
Love is patient and is kind. Love
doesn't envy. Love doesn't brag,
is not proud, doesn't behave itself
inappropriately, doesn't seek its own
way, is not provoked, takes no account of
evil; doesn't rejoice in unrighteousness,
but rejoices with the truth; bears all
things, believes all things, hopes
all things, and endures
all things.

LOVE

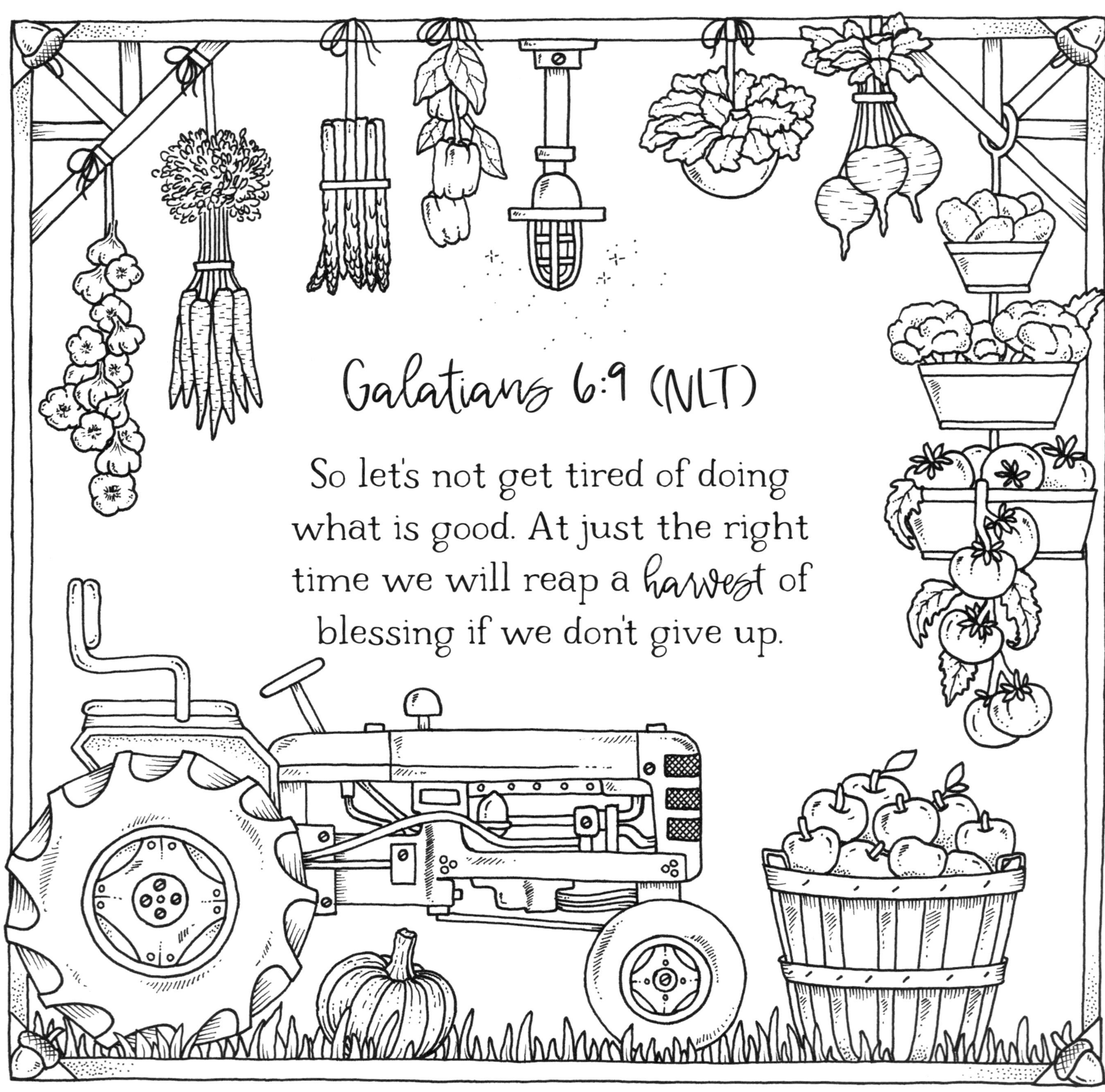
Galatians 6:9 (NLT)
So let's not get tired of doing what is good. At just the right time we will reap a harvest of blessing if we don't give up.

harvest

Psalm 146:5–6 (NLV)
Happy is he whose help is the God of Jacob, and whose hope is in the Lord his God. The Lord made heaven and earth, the sea and all that is in them. He is faithful forever.

HAPPY

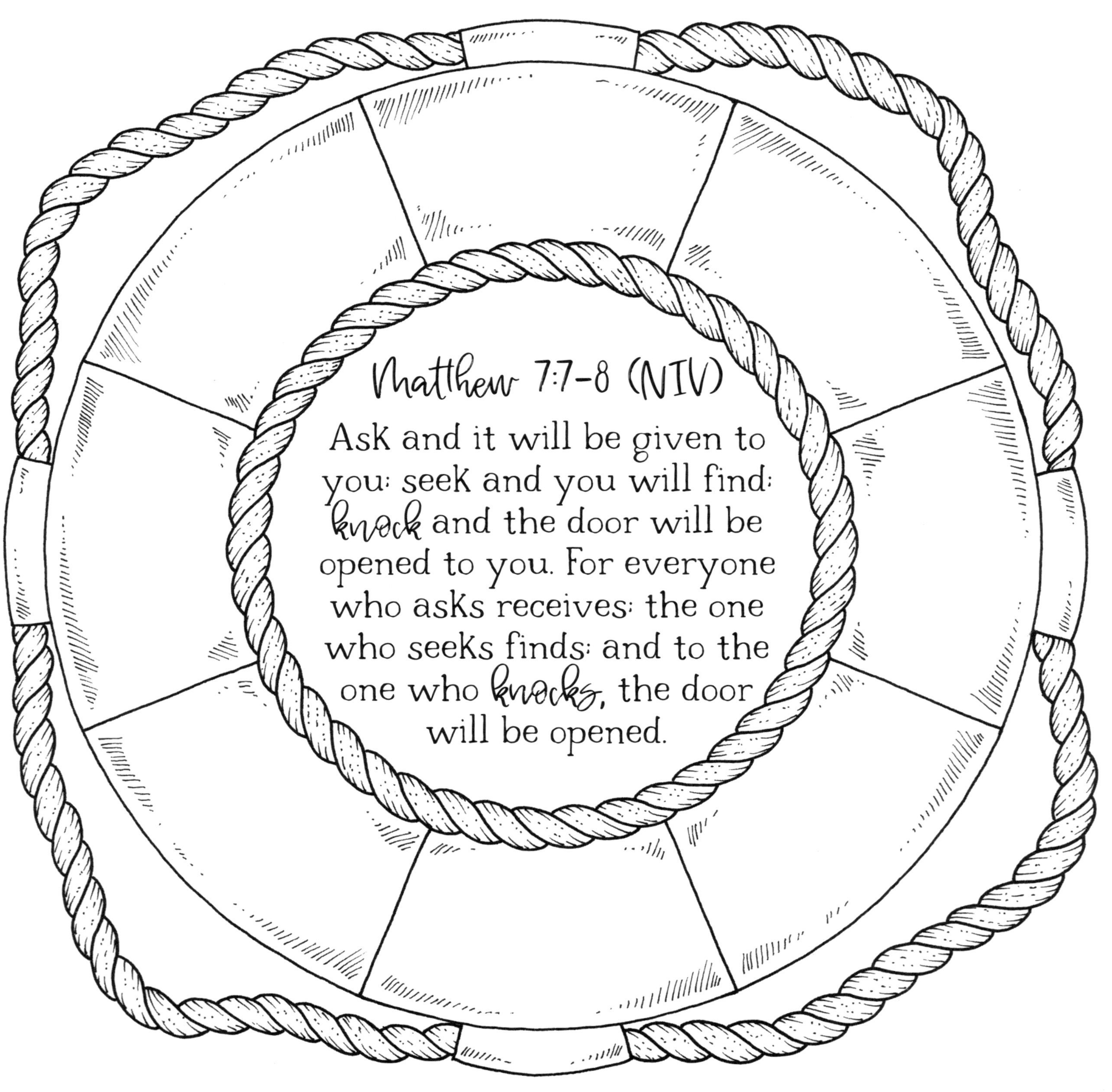
Matthew 7:7-8 (NIV)
Ask and it will be given to
you; seek and you will find;
knock and the door will be
opened to you. For everyone
who asks receives; the one
who seeks finds; and to the
one who knocks, the door
will be opened.

KNOCK

Isaiah 40:8 (WEB)
The grass withers,
the flower fades:
but the word of our
God stands forever.

HOLY
BIBLE
FOREVER

GOD'S WAY
Proverbs 3:5–6 (NKJV)
Trust in the Lord with all your heart, And lean not on your own understanding;
In all your ways acknowledge Him, And He shall direct your paths.
YOUR WAY
OUR WAY
HIS WAY
HER WAY

TRUST

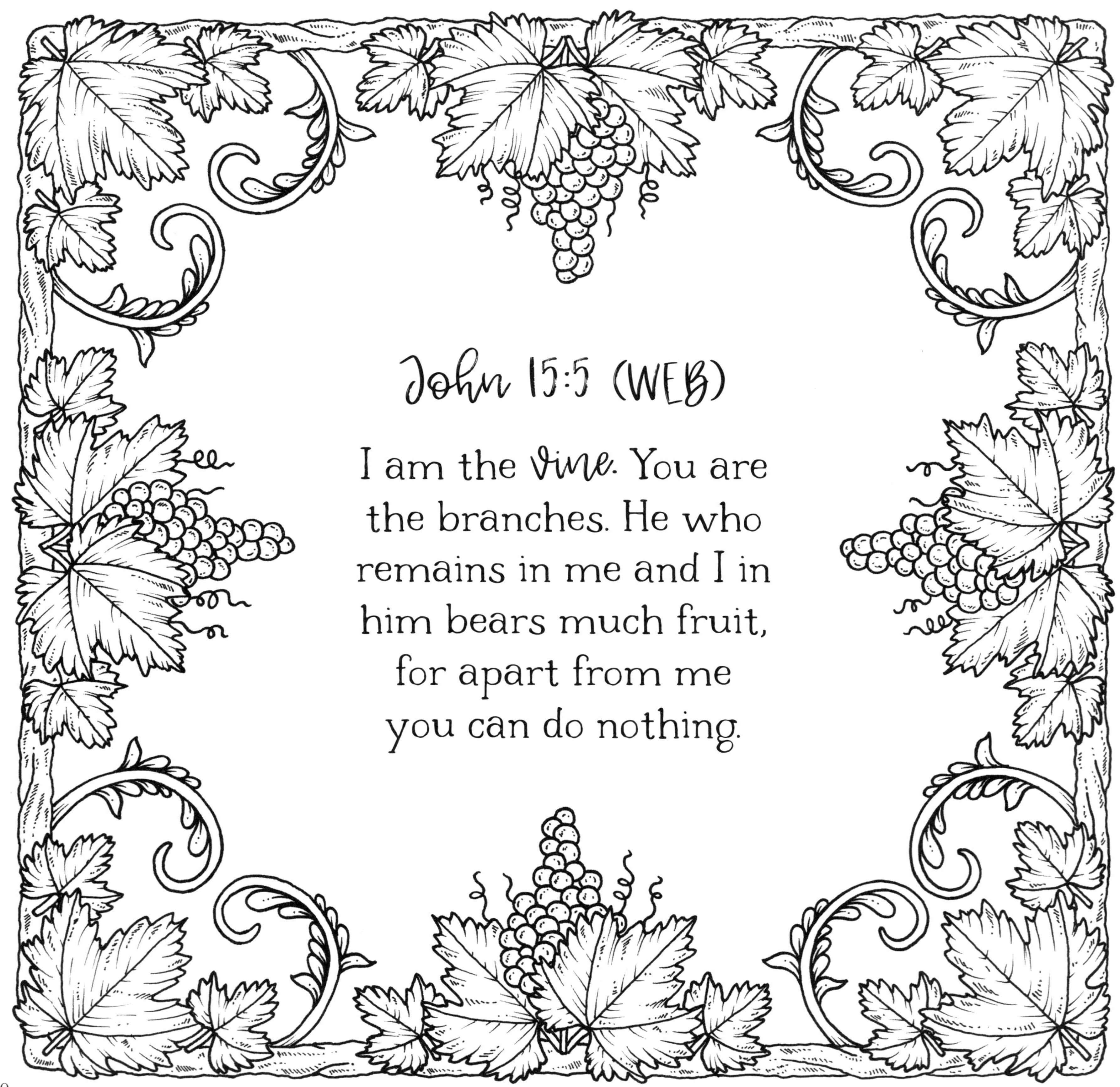
John 15:5 (WEB)
I am the vine. You are the branches. He who remains in me and I in him bears much fruit, for apart from me you can do nothing.

Vine

Psalm 95:1-2 (ESV)
Oh come, let us sing to the
Lord; let us make a joyful noise
to the rock of our salvation! Let
us come into his presence with
thanksgiving; let us make a
joyful noise to him with
songs of praise!

sing

Lamentations 3:22-23 (ESV)
The steadfast love of
the Lord never ceases;
his mercies never come
to an end; they are new
every morning; great is
your faithfulness.

mercies

Proverbs 18:10 (ESV)
The name of the Lord
is a strong tower; the
righteous man runs into
it and is safe.

TOWER

Matthew 6:31-33 (ESV)
Therefore do not be anxious, saying "What shall we eat?" or "What shall we drink?" or "What shall we wear?" For the Gentiles seek after all these things, and your heavenly Father knows that you need them all. But seek first the kingdom of God and his righteousness, and all these things will be added to you.

SEEK

Psalm 139:9-10 (WEB)
If I take the wings of the
dawn, and settle in the
uttermost parts of the sea,
even there your hand will
lead me, and your right
hand will hold me.

LEAD

Ezekiel 36:26-27 (ESV)
And I will give you a new heart,
and a new spirit I will put
within you. And I will remove
the heart of stone from your
flesh and give you a heart of
flesh. And I will put my spirit
within you, and cause you to
walk in my statutes and be
careful to obey my rules.

SPIRIT

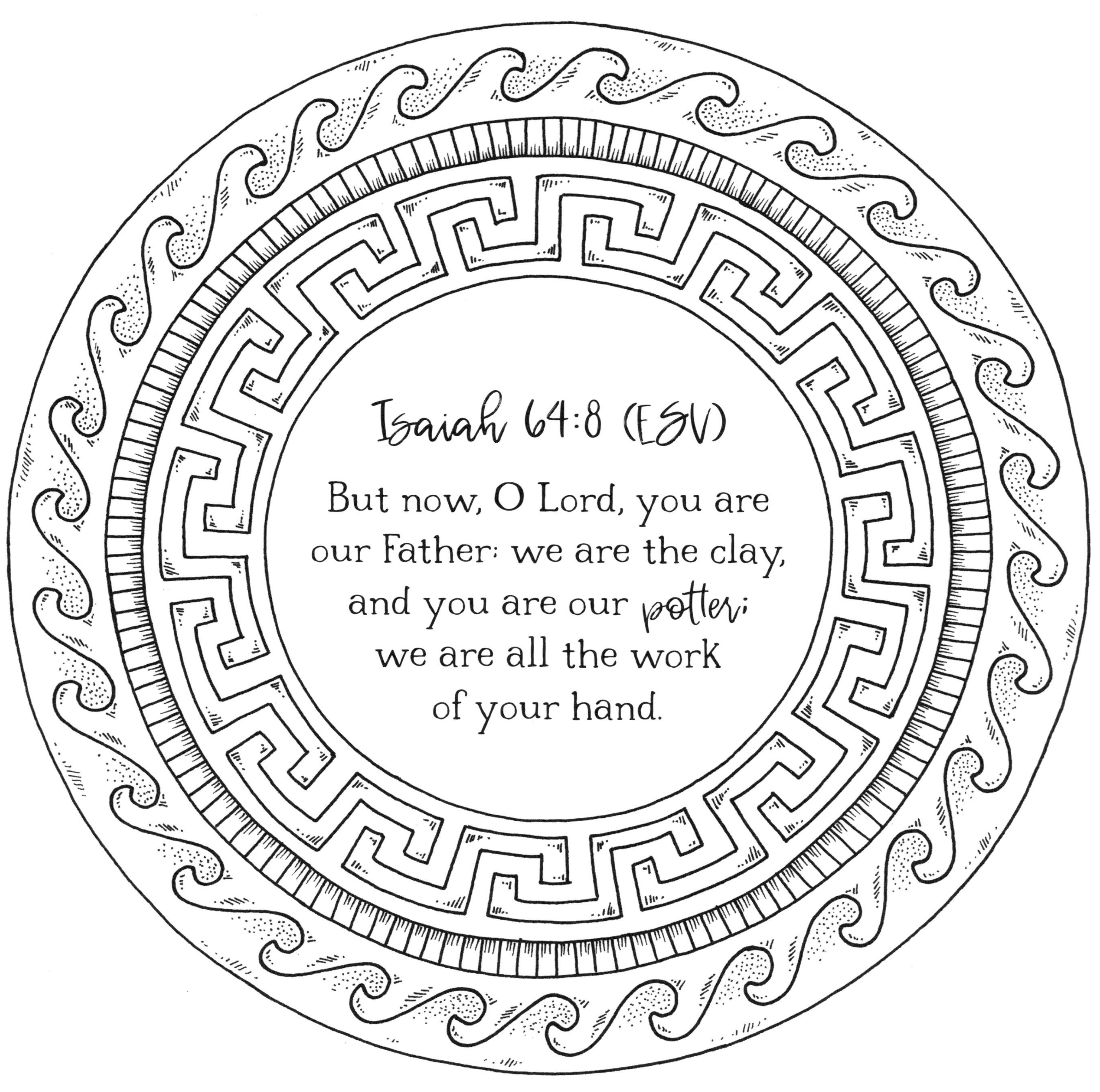
Isaiah 64:8 (ESV)
But now, O Lord, you are
our Father; we are the clay,
and you are our potter;
we are all the work
of your hand.

POTTER

Matthew 11:28 (NIV)
Come to me, all you
who are weary and
burdened, and I will
give you rest.

REST

Matthew 28:5-7 (WEB)
The angel answered the women,
"Don't be afraid, for I know that you
seek Jesus, who has been crucified. He
is not here, for he has risen, just like
he said. Come, see the place where the
Lord was lying. Go quickly and tell his
disciples, 'He has risen from the dead,
and behold, he goes before you into
Galilee; there you will see him.'
Behold, I have told you."

RISEN

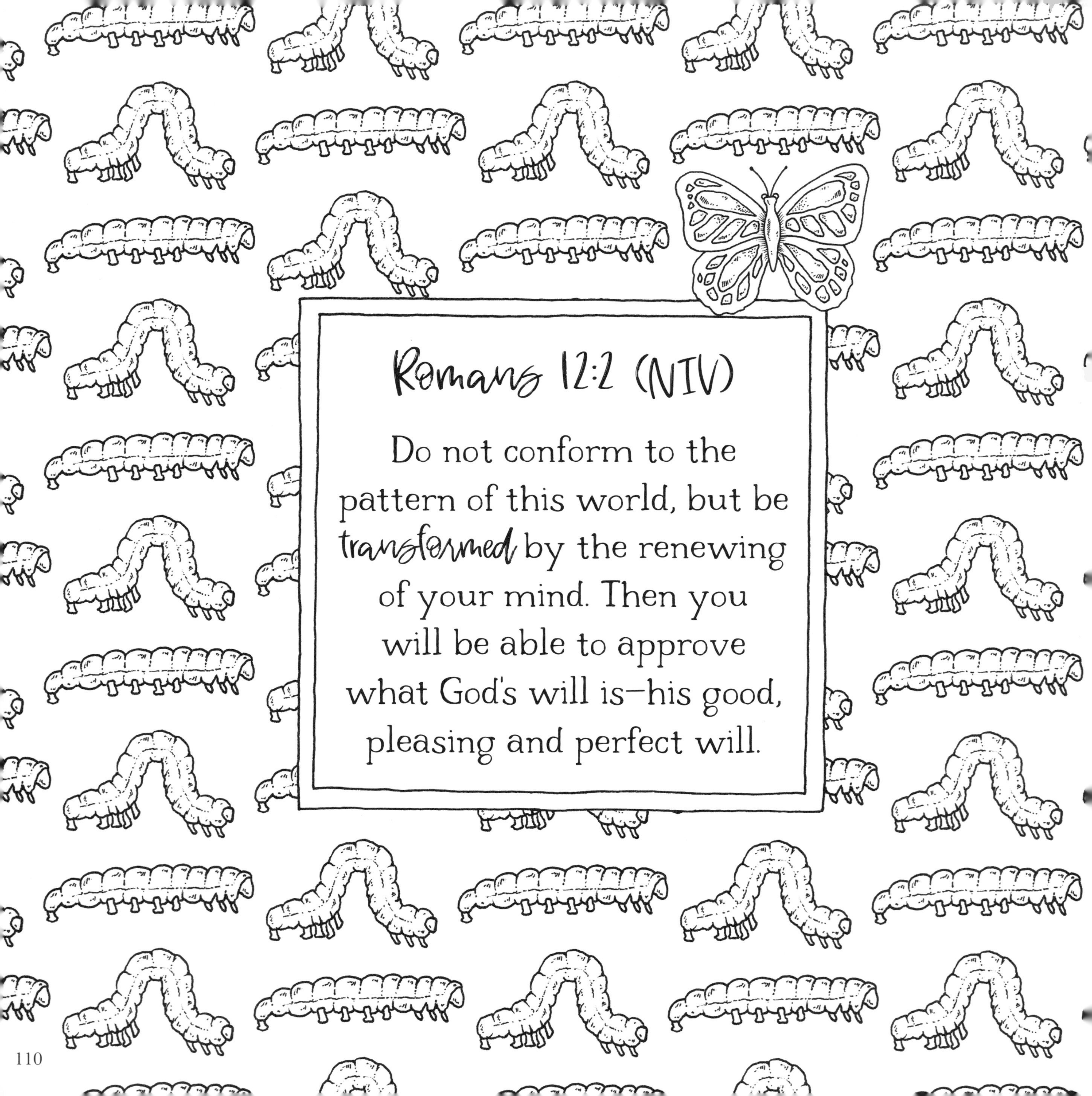
Romans 12:2 (NIV)
Do not conform to the pattern of this world, but be transformed by the renewing of your mind. Then you will be able to approve what God's will is—his good, pleasing and perfect will.

TRANSFORMED

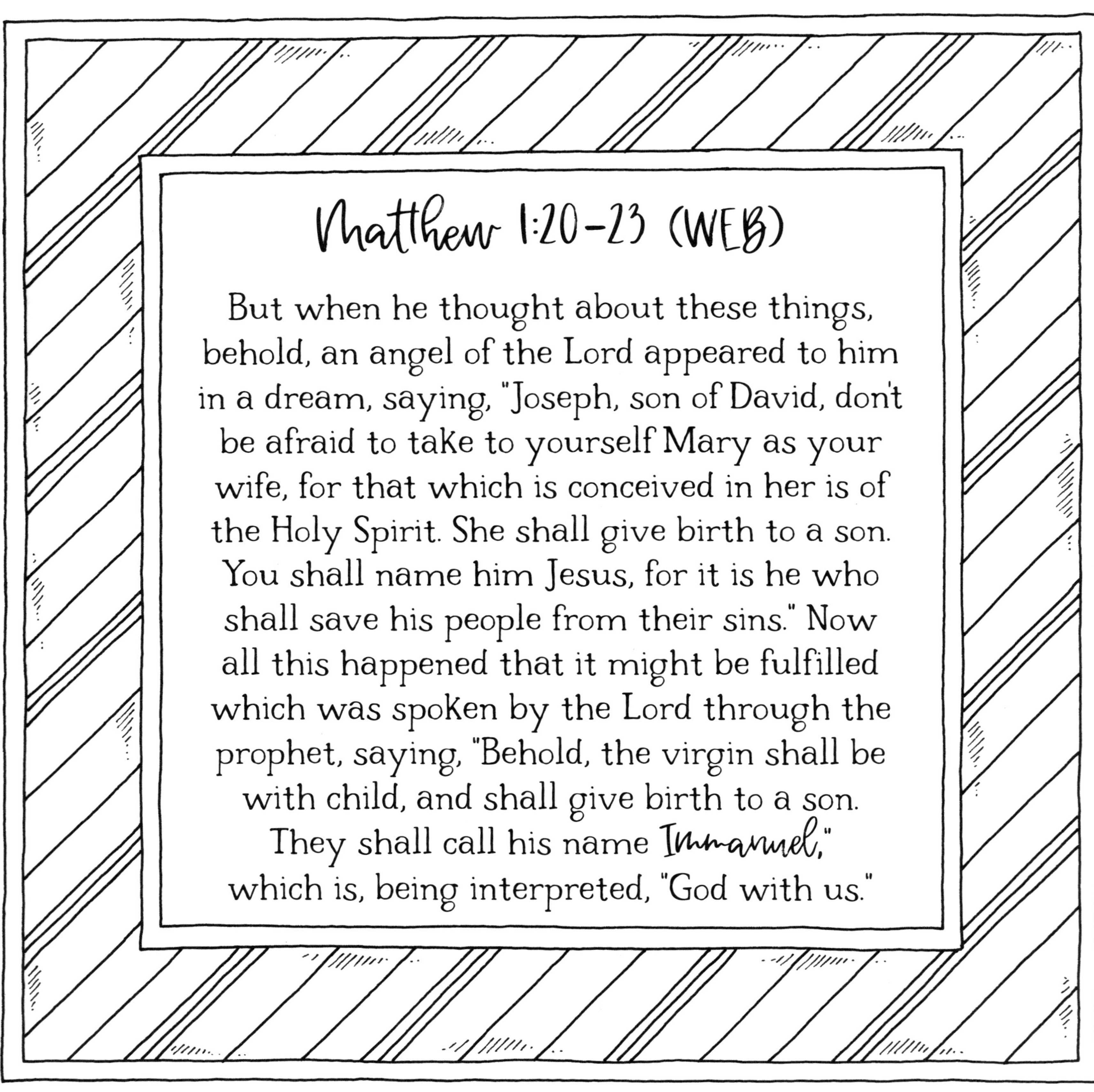

Matthew 1:20–23 (WEB)

But when he thought about these things, behold, an angel of the Lord appeared to him in a dream, saying, "Joseph, son of David, don't be afraid to take to yourself Mary as your wife, for that which is conceived in her is of the Holy Spirit. She shall give birth to a son. You shall name him Jesus, for it is he who shall save his people from their sins." Now all this happened that it might be fulfilled which was spoken by the Lord through the prophet, saying, "Behold, the virgin shall be with child, and shall give birth to a son. They shall call his name Immanuel," which is, being interpreted, "God with us."

Immanuel

the end
BIBLE

Color Test Page

Color Test Page

Acknowledgments

First and foremost, I want to thank God for the inspiration and abilities He's blessed me with to draw and create this book. I give all the glory to Him and He deserves all the praise! It has been my hope to create a tool for memorizing Scripture that both honors and serves Him, and none of this would be possible without the gifts He's given and allowed me to use. To John, thank you for your patience and support as I drew the pages of this book. I know it was a long process, and there were many late nights and countless times that you stepped up to cover for me so I could draw. Thank you for believing in me and your support! I love you! Skylar, Asher, & Baylor, you three inspire me more than words can say. You are my greatest treasure in life and bring me such joy! I thank God for allowing me the privilege to be your mama, and I hope you know how loved and cherished you are! Dad & Mom, thank you for your words of wisdom and steady support. I love you both so much and have valued your input throughout the entire process of creating this! Heather, the best sister anyone could ask for, thank you for being the outlet I could share my drawings with and for your patience for the millions of texts and images I sent you as I created new pages for this book. To Rob, this partnership with CA Gifts wouldn't be possible without you! Your kindness, professionalism, and patience has been top notch, and I cannot thank you enough. Thank you for believing in the possibilities for this book and for the opportunity to work with CA Gifts! To everyone who had a hand in this book at CA Gifts, thank you!

Other Titles

To learn more about Shannon's other titles, including retailer info and new releases, please scan the QR code with your smart phone or visit her website shannonroberts.com/collections/books.

Prayer Journal for Women

Prayer Journal for Teen Girls

Chalk It Up To Grace

Shannon is a wife and mother of three with a passion for spreading God's word and the good news of Jesus. She has been drawing and lettering professionally since 2014 after leaving her teaching career to be a stay-at-home mom. What started as a side hustle, while staying home caring for her young children at the time, quickly turned into a full-time art business. Since then, her work has been featured worldwide and sold globally through the companies and businesses she partners with. Her best-selling book *Prayer Journal For Women* has sold over 1 million copies worldwide and has been translated into multiple languages. She has a passion for family and enjoys staying active with them outdoors. To learn more about Shannon and her work, you can visit her websites shannonroberts.com and thewhitelime.etsy.com.